Brush Lettering

WORKBOOK

LEARN 9 BRUSH LETTERING ALPHABETS

PETER PAUPER PRESS, INC.
WHITE PLAINS, NEW YORK

PETER PAUPER PRESS
Fine Books and Gifts Since 1928

OUR COMPANY

In 1928, at the age of twenty-two, Peter Beilenson began printing books on a small press in the basement of his parents' home in Larchmont, New York. Peter—and later, his wife, Edna—sought to create fine books that sold at "prices even a pauper could afford."

Today, still family owned and operated, Peter Pauper Press continues to honor our founders' legacy—and our customers' expectations—of beauty, quality, and value.

Designed by Heather Zschock

Copyright © 2019
Peter Pauper Press, Inc.
202 Mamaroneck Avenue
White Plains, NY 10601 USA
All rights reserved
ISBN 978-1-4413-3118-2
Printed in China
7 6 5 4 3 2

Visit us at www.peterpauper.com

Table of Contents

How to use this workbook...

To achieve the contrasting thin and thick lines that give brush calligraphy its elegant look, follow the rule of **thin upstrokes** and **thick downstrokes.** Pressing down lightly with your brush pen creates a thin line, while pressing down harder creates a thick line.

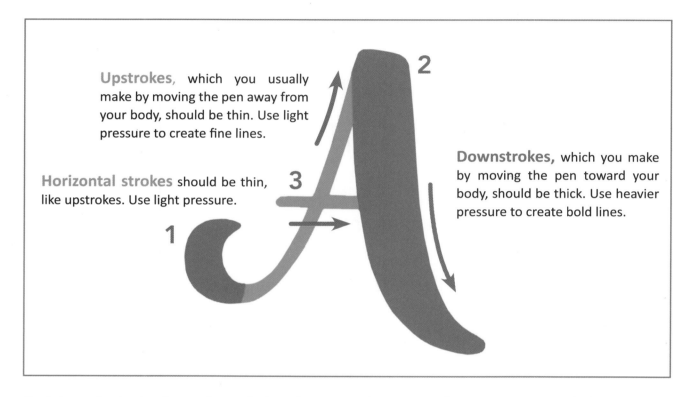

Upstrokes, which you usually make by moving the pen away from your body, should be thin. Use light pressure to create fine lines.

Horizontal strokes should be thin, like upstrokes. Use light pressure.

Downstrokes, which you make by moving the pen toward your body, should be thick. Use heavier pressure to create bold lines.

Each letter in the book is color-coded to show you where to use heavy pressure, and where to use light pressure.

Green strokes are light pressure strokes, usually upstrokes or horizontal strokes. You may also use continuous light pressure for extra flourishes that decorate a letter.

Purple strokes strokes are heavy pressure strokes. These are always downstrokes.

Follow the order of the numbers to create the strokes. The placement of each number shows you where to start each stroke.

When creating **flourishes**—extra swirls and decorations on a letter—you may sometimes keep your line thin, and your pressure light, even when making downstrokes. You may also use a tiny downstroke to join a heavier **dot**, or droplet shape, to the end of a thin upstroke as decoration. Always avoid thick upstrokes, though, as they can damage your brush pen.

1. **Flip through and pick an alphabet.** Three of the alphabets in this book are sized for large brush pens, and six are best with small brush pens. Choose an alphabet that works for the size of the pen you're using. (Try drawing thick and thin strokes with your pen if you're not sure.) If you're new to brush lettering, try starting with the first large brush pen alphabet.

2. **Trace the first grayed-out letter.** Create your strokes in the order indicated by the numbers. Use light pressure where you see green, and heavier pressure where you see purple.

3. **Try the letter yourself in the practice space.** Draw the strokes in the same order every time.

4. **Work your way through the alphabet.** Then, try your hand at numbers and punctuation marks.

5. **Try joining letters and combining alphabets.** At the end of the large and small brush pen sections, you'll find traceable words and phrases that demonstrate ways of linking letters and mixing styles.

6. **Try it on your own!**

A A

a a

B B

b b

C C

c c

D D

d d

E E

e e

F F

f f

G G g g

JE JE h h

J J i i

J J j j

K K K K

L L L L

m m m m

N N n n

O O o o

p p p p

Q Q q q

R R r r

S S s s

T T t t

u u u u

V V v v

w w w w

X X x x

y y y y

z z z z

0 0 1 1 2 2

3 3 4 4 5 5

6 6 7 7 8 8

9 9 ! ! & &

A A A

a a

B B B

b b

C C C

c c

D D D

d d

E E E

e e

F F F

f f

$\mathcal{G}^{2}$ $\mathcal{G}$

$\mathcal{H}^{1}_{2}$ $\mathcal{H}$

$\mathcal{J}$ $\mathcal{J}$

$\mathcal{J}^{2}_{1}$ $\mathcal{J}$

$\mathcal{K}^{2}_{3}$ $\mathcal{K}$

$\mathcal{L}_{1}$ $\mathcal{L}$

$g^{1}{}^{2}$ g

h^{1}_{2} h

i^{2}_{1} i

j^{2}_{1} j

k^{1}_{2} k

l_{1} l

19

$\mathcal{M}$ $\mathcal{M}$ m m

$\mathcal{N}$ $\mathcal{N}$ n n

$\mathcal{O}$ $\mathcal{O}$ o o

$\mathcal{P}$ $\mathcal{P}$ p p

$\mathcal{Q}$ $\mathcal{Q}$ q q

$\mathcal{R}$ $\mathcal{R}$ r r

S S   s s

T T   t t

U U   u u

V V   v v

W W   w w

X X   x x

Y Y y y

Z Z z

0 0 1 1 2 2

3 3 4 4 5 5

6 6 7 7 8 8

9 9 ! ! ? ?

2
A A A A
3

2
B B B B
3

2 1
C C C C

2
D D D D

2
1 E E E E
3

2
F F F F
3

G G G G

H H H H

I I I I

J J J J

K K K K

L L L L

M M M M M

N N N N N

O O O O O

P P P P P

Q Q Q Q Q

R R R R R

S S S S

T T T T

u u u u

V V V V

W W W W

X X X X

y ²y y y y

¹z ²z z z z
³

¹0 0 ¹|| ¹²2 2

¹3 3 ¹4 4 ²¹5 5
²   ²   ³
³

¹6 6 ²¹7 7 ¹8 8
²

¹9 9 ¹|! ²¹&&
¹   ³
●² ²
⁴
⁵

Adventure awaits!

you are so LOVED

REACH for the Moon

Happy Birthday

Thank you

Follow your star

Believe
in
Yourself

DREAM
BIG!

Grateful

$\mathcal{H}^2_1$ $\mathcal{H}$

$h^1_2 h$

$\mathcal{I}_1 \mathcal{I}$

•2
$i_1 i$

$\mathcal{J}_1 \mathcal{J}$

•2
$j_1 j$

$\mathcal{K}^2_{13} \mathcal{K}$

$k^1_{23} k$

$\mathcal{L}_1 \mathcal{L}$

$\ell_1 \ell$

$\mathcal{M}^2_{13} \mathcal{M}$

$m^1_{23} m$

$\mathcal{N}^2_1 \mathcal{N}$

$n^1_2 n$

$\mathcal{V}$ $\mathcal{V}$ $\mathcal{V}$ $\mathcal{W}$ $\mathcal{W}$

$\mathcal{W}$ $\mathcal{W}$ $\mathcal{W}$ $\mathcal{W}$ $\mathcal{W}$

$\mathcal{X}$ $\mathcal{X}$ x x

$\mathcal{Y}$ $\mathcal{Y}$ y y

$\mathcal{Z}$ $\mathcal{Z}$ z z

0 0 1 1 2 2 3 3 4 4

5 5 6 6 7 7 8 8 9 9

$_2h$ h

$_2i$ i

$^2\!j^1$ j

^2k k
$_2$ $_3$

ℓ ℓ
$_1$

^1m m
$_2$ $_3$

^1n n
$_2$

O O   o o

P P   p p

Q Q   q q

R R   r r

S S   s s

T T   t t

U U   u u

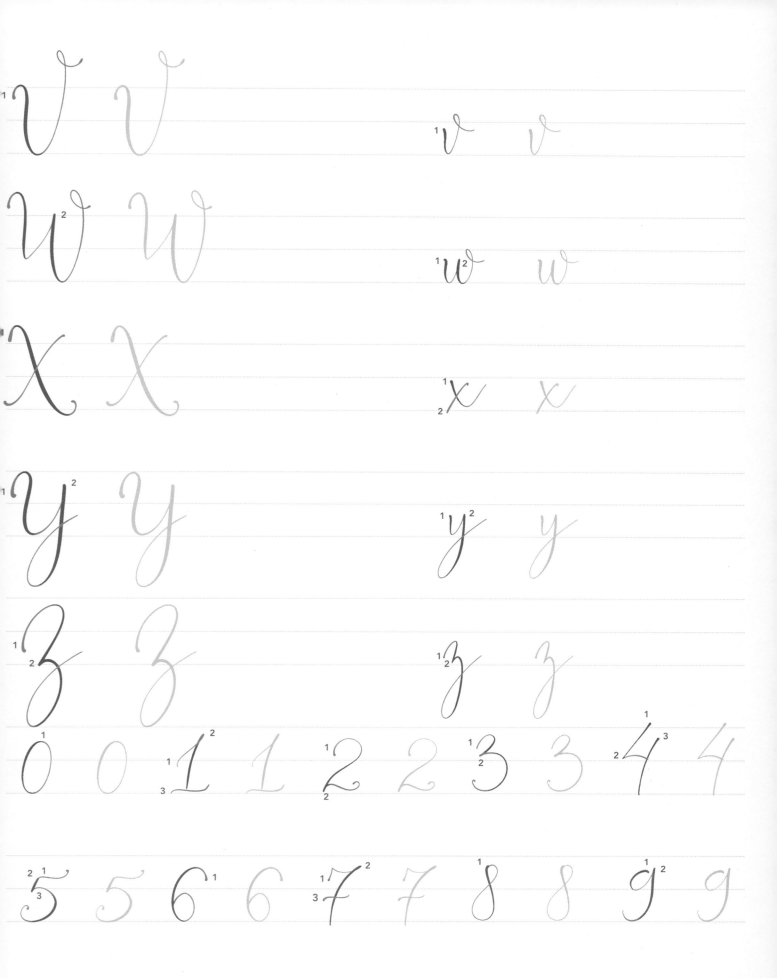

$\mathcal{H}$ $\mathcal{H}$ h h

$\mathcal{I}$ $\mathcal{I}$ i i

$\mathcal{J}$ $\mathcal{J}$ j j

$\mathcal{K}$ $\mathcal{K}$ k k

$\mathcal{L}$ $\mathcal{L}$ l l

$\mathcal{M}$ $\mathcal{M}$ m m

$\mathcal{N}$ $\mathcal{N}$ n n

V V   v v

W W   w w

X X   x x

Y Y   y y

L L   z z

0 0   1 1   2 2   3 3   4 4

5 5   6 6   7 7   8 8   9 9

$\mathcal{H}$ ¹ $\mathcal{H}$ ² $\mathcal{H}$

h h

$\mathcal{G}$ ¹ $\mathcal{G}$

i i

$\mathcal{G}$ ¹ $\mathcal{G}$

j j

$\mathcal{K}$ ¹ ² ³ $\mathcal{K}$

k k

$\mathcal{L}$ ¹ ² $\mathcal{L}$

l l

$\mathcal{M}$ ¹ ² ³ $\mathcal{M}$

m m

$\mathcal{N}$ ¹ ² $\mathcal{N}$

n n

O O   o o

P P   p p

Q Q   q q

R R   r r

S S   s s

T T   t t

U U   u u

V V v v

W W w w

X X x x

Y Y y y

Z Z z z

0 0 0 1 1 1 2 2 2 3 3 3 4 4 4

5 5 6 6 7 7 8 8 9 9

A A A A A

B B B B B

C C C C C

D D D D D

E E E E E

F F F F F

G G G G G

H H H H H H

I I I I I I

J J J J J J

K K K K K K

L L L L L L

M M M M M M

N N N N N N

O O O O O

P P P P P

Q Q Q Q Q

R R R R R

S S S S S

T T T T T

U U U U U

V V V V V

W W W W W

X X X X X

y y y y y

1 1 1 1 1

0 0 1 1 2 2 3 3 4 4

5 5 6 6 7 7 8 8 9 9

A A A A A

B B B B B

C C C C C

D D D D D

E E E E E

F F F F F

G G G G G

H H H H H

I I I I I

J J J J J

K K K K K

L L L L L

M M M M M

N N N N N

O O O O O

P P P P P

Q Q Q Q Q

R R R R R

S S S S S

T T T T T

U U U U U

V V V V V

W W W W W

X X X X X

y y y y y

Z Z Z Z Z

0 0 1 1 2 2 3 3 4 4

5 5 6 6 7 7 8 8 9 9

Live

Choose

LOVE Laugh

JOY

Be-YOU-tiful

Congratulations

Thank you

Happy BIRTHDAY

Cheers!

WOW!

Better Together

DARE to DREAM

Be UNSTOPPABLE

THROW Kindness AROUND LIKE Confetti

HAPPY Holidays

Work hard
STAY HUMBLE
Be kind

ONE day AT A time

ADVENTURE awaits ♡